STRATNAV: The Law of Propulsion

STRATNAV: The Law of Propulsion
ISBN: 979-8-59-266544-8

First published in Great Britain
in 2021 through Amazon self-publishing
service Kindle Direct Publishing

Typeset in the UK at The Joy of Pages
www.thejoyofpages.co.uk

This book is dedicated to my daughter Lucy; I love you very much. You are an inspiration. You have achieved great things and are destined for a great and compelling future.

"Logic will get you from A to B.
Imagination will take you everywhere."

Albert Einstein

CONTENTS

ACKNOWLEDGEMENTS

Lucy: my daughter and inspiration.

Michael Heppell and Write That Book Master Class 2020.

WTB2020 Buddy Group: Lucas Vigilante, Karen Balmond, Donna Clark, Paul Limb and Deborah Simmons and KC Moi.

Jonathan MacDonald: The world's greatest thinker and creator of *Powered by Change*. Writer of *The Rise of Advanced Thought: How to Train your Thinking to Achieve Almost Anything.*

Adrian Hawkins: Founder of biz4Biz

Jo Clarke: For enlightening me to the true meaning of Mindfulness https://www.innerspaceworks.com/.

The women that taught me the meaning of feminine energy. You know who you are.

David Hambling for his publishing advice, editorial and typesetting of this book.

viii

FOREWORD

by Jonathon Macdonald
Winner of the Business
Book Award 2019

Very occasionally I read a set of text that transports me to another dimension. For example, I remember the first time I read about Narnia, my dreams were populated by alternative realities from that day onward. I remember coming across The Cluetrain Manifesto and feeling the same way. I have realised it is not the length of the script, nor the format it adopts, that captures me the most. Indeed, there are some manuscripts that require several hundred pages to adequately describe the thesis, and others with few pages that have profound impact. *StratNav* is the latter. And it is to your benefit that you are about to embark on this journey.

Merging Western business methodologies with Eastern philosophies, *StratNav* achieves a rare thing - the ability to bridge the old and new in a futuristic yet historic way. It is an accompaniment to the most experienced business person, whilst also being a launchpad for one's first endeavours into a new arena.

When I first read *StratNav*, I called Richard immediately and grilled him with questions. I wanted to know how the structure had taken shape and what the edges of his thinking were. I wanted to know how his experiences resulted in the content you physically or digitally have before you today. Ultimately, I wanted to know how a collection of thought such as this could transcend most other modern publications of thought, and enter into the lofty heights of genuine thought leadership.

Richard is far too modest to either claim or entertain such status. So I'm taking this opportunity to do so instead.

StratNav is the type of thinking that changes paradigms. It is unique, accessible yet profound. *StratNav* is the type of thinking that inspires me to achieve more and remember that I am still a student. *StratNav* is the type of thinking the world needs right now. I'm tremendously honoured to have the permission to be at least a minor part of it.

Jonathan MacDonald Winner of the Business Book Award 2019 (Embracing Change).

Powered By Change (PBC) is the most advanced, comprehensive and powerful business growth platform ever created. PBC is based on the *Sunday Times* Bestselling book, *Powered By Change*, and its methodologies have been incorporated into hundreds of companies all over the world, from startups to multi-billion dollar blue-chip organisations.

FOREWORD

by Adrian Hawkins OBE
Founder of biz4Biz

It's a common mistake. You start a business, to create a new lifestyle for you and your family, and at the beginning earning a living is the only purpose in life. By the time you are reading this book, this mission has been accomplished and you are seeking the opportunity to do things rather differently, or you have not realised that change is possible and hopefully this book is opening your mind to the possibility of change.

StratNav and its connection with *Powered by Change*, should open your eyes to the art of the possible.

There are roads to greater success that exist and setting the correct destination is all important to finding the right roads and the shortest journey to take to your destination. It takes a while to recognise that the lifestyle and the initial objectives are safe, but then the eureka moment happens and you suddenly realise that you are in control of your own destiny and that you should make the best use of the opportunity.

Building a business to become more powerful and profit generative is a fun thing to do and will provide a valuable return on your investment in both time and energy. *StratNav* can make this process much quicker, and that part is very important. The speed of change can also free up valuable time for you and the family.

Remember, strategic growth is positive for your bottom line, it will reduce the stress of running a business and it has the potential to significantly embellish your lifestyle.

Work smarter and not harder with *StratNav*.

STRATNAV

THE LAW OF PROPULSION

RICHARD PERRY

WELCOME TO STRATNAV

It's Time for a Re-Evolution

It's time to fire up the StratNav! It's already within you; have you noticed? It's listening, working and waiting. What story are you telling it about the future? Where you are today was once a destination you put into your StratNav. You may not have realised it at the time.

This book will give you a powerful gift. The gift of awareness and understanding so that you may propel yourself to a destination you choose. Think of this book as an introduction to a new lexicon of success. It provides concepts and language to help you design the future. Once you are familiar with the idea you will be able to take the next step in your journey with us.

Believing is Seeing. It's up to you to create the compelling future you want. Yes, it is based on purpose but more importantly, it is one you will create 'on purpose.' And now is the time to start. *StratNav* is there to guide you and help you to decide what you pay attention to. They say you attract what you are, so why not decide what you are and understand how to control that so you move from attraction to propulsion?

Take one mind, invite the soul and add some emotion and intellect. You will need these elements to create a compelling future, define a path and propel yourself to the end point like a Time Lord. All good Time Lords have a time machine and that is what *StratNav* gives you.

It's what Strategy Buddha calls Perpetual Coherence; a continuous state of flow that combines body and mind together to focus on achieving your goals.

Add that explosive mix into the StratNav and you have your very own time machine to ensure you have a whole new experience of time that will drive you forward like never before.

Are you ready for the ride of your life? Here's your invitation.

AN INVITATION
TO THE FUTURE

Dear Fellow Traveller,

Have you ever wondered why things never really turned out the way you thought in business or life?

Well, what if 'the way you thought' was the problem? What if, without realising it, you had programmed your internal guidance system and ended up exactly where you asked it to take you?

If you are curious right now, then you are ready to enter the world of the StratNav and take your first steps into the courage zone...Think of your brain like a time machine, enabling you to engage in a sort of time travel where you can test out various compelling futures or even revisit the past. The StratNav enables you to be a Time Lord.

It's a Strategy Warp. A quantum process that gets you to the destination rapidly—think of it as a hyper-loop. A high speed vehicle that moves at 700km/hr in a frictionless tunnel.

StratNav is your answer to true strategic thinking and freedom. It's a re-evolution of all things strategic. At its core is the ability to optimise your skill of creativity and apply to a higher purpose.

You will benefit from the most important ROI there is: Return on Intellect. Better still, *StratNav* will enable you to overcome that other major risk: Risk of Inaction. Once you learn what is possible then you will no longer see it as a risk.

You will be given a whole new lexicon to enable you to speak the language of the StratNav and engage with other tribe members.

Perhaps you are like me and not in the 'box.' Or perhaps you are ready to escape from the box and need some help to emerge and reach your potential.

In the courage zone you'll need the rocket fuel of intellect, emotion, empathy, spirituality, and grit. You are going to need more than emotional intelligence. Welcome to the world of the intelligent use of emotion. Once you've learned to create your emotions rather than be controlled by them you are ready to enter the world of the StratNav. As the CEO of NeuroGym, John Assaraf, would say, "Are you using your brain or is your brain using you?"

StratNav will bring feminine energy to its rightful place so that there is balance in your approach.

You are in control, you have the destination and you have the guidance system. It's a mix of logic, masculine and feminine energy, creativity and spirituality and it makes you feel more human.

I'll sign off with some words that capture how I think and feel. Use them if you wish or create your own. Either way, you'll need a mantra to guide you. It's not an empty 'strapline', it's pure strategic energy:

"I am nothing without my past, I live in the present, yet I am everything with my future."

Yours,
Richard Perry

Guardian of the StratNav & Disciple of the Strategy Buddha.

They say, "put your mind to it," well the Strategy Buddha says, "put your heart and mind to it."

Remember:

MINDSET: TOOLSET: GET SET

If you've spent years in business and have tried numerous things to transform yourself and your business then let me assure you that you are now in possession of the most powerful thing you've ever known. If I sound like Indiana Jones in search of the Holy Grail, I make no apologies. *StratNav* is the ultimate combination of intellect and energy. You will be licensed to use it and the Strategy Buddha will help you make the grade.

StratNav, as well as being a framework, is real. It is a physical part of your body that requires fuel, chemicals, hormones and voltage, which is carefully integrated into your brain. Yet at the same time it is energy, ideas, inspiration, a laser beam and a propellant. It's your RAS, or your Reticular Activating System, and it's your gut feeling. A gut feeling based on experience and insight. Once you have mastered it you will be ready to learn about strategic thinking, planning and implementation. It's a new framework for a new type of business model.

You have my permission to be creative, inspired, energised and incredible. Once you have mastered the StratNav you will be better placed to appreciate the range of tools in the strategic pragmatist's kitbag.

As you explore the book I will tell you the secret behind the StratNav—it takes many forms.

Which form it takes will depend on you. If you are ready to fire up the StratNav then let's begin.

WHAT IS STRATNAV?

Just like a real-life satnav you might use in your car, part of the StratNav exists in a physical form.

In fact, we've known about it for thousands of years and did not have the brain science to be able to prove it. Just read a few quotes from the great minds of the past:

"The world is but a canvas
to our imagination."

Thoreau

"Be the kind of person that you
want people to think you are."

Socrates

"The future influences the present
just as much as the past."

Friedrich Nietzsche

"Whatever the mind can conceive
and believe the body can achieve."

Napoleon Hill

"Believing is Seeing."

Dr. Lisa Feldman Barrett

"The best way to predict the
future is to create it."

Peter Drucker

Strategy Buddha says this:

"When you truly want something and go after it without limiting yourself with disbelief, the Universe will help you to make it happen." (This is the law of attraction concept by William Walker Atkinson.)

"The secret of your future is hidden in your daily routine."

It's the basis of the great work of James Clear who wrote *Atomic Habits*. It is this link between the present and a compelling future that is vital to the StratNav.

Strategy Buddha believes that: 'believing is seeing.'

Strategy Buddha gives you The Law of Propulsion

You are now ready to discover where the StratNav can be found because you are ready to seek it out and you will be ready to use it by the time you have read the book.

StratNav

This book will introduce you to the StratNav. It's something you already possess and for many it may have been taking you to the wrong place... and fast. In fact, it may have taken you on the wrong path many times and you were not even aware. If you retain the programming, then you are destined to repeat the same behaviours and you'll get the same results. In fact, Einstein touched on this when he said that, "The definition of insanity is doing the same thing over and over again and expecting a different result."

What if you didn't realise you were doing the same thing? What if you could do the right thing every time? What if it is possible to do things and know you will get a result? It's a neurological algorithm to reach a compelling future.

StratNav will guide you through a creative, emotional and structured method of changing your code. *StratNav* is about being more human not less. What distinguishes this book from others is that it avoids the false safety of the strategic toolkit. There are numerous models and methodologies which are attractive to the unaware. They will help you identify the issues of a market, a sector or an industry. You will however still be guided by a StratNav that is not optimised. It will lead you to create, plan and select strategies that are likely to fail.

A faulty guidance system will get you nowhere fast.

StratNav defines who you are at any point in time. It can feel like a weight or it can move you at warp speed.

When you are guided by your StratNav you will discover your inner genius. That feeling that you are on the right track, going the right way and that great feeling that people describe when they say, "it just feels right." We

12

hear about your 'gut' as your 'second brain' and it's interesting that 90% of serotonin is found in the gut. It's the optimism drug. It's a place of 'flow.'

Strategic thinking is about shaping the future of your business. It's about you as a leader and it's about the team. Strategy is about winning. This means it's creative, pragmatic, intellectual and challenging. It's about grit and determination to execute but also having the wisdom to alter course in the face of reality. *StratNav* brings soul and spirituality into the picture.

StratNav is a way of life

StratNav is a new way of thinking about thinking, behaving and being. As you learn how to master the process the StratNav will get better. If we talk about machine learning in Artificial Intelligence, we get to our equivalent… Actual Intelligence with human learning. The combination of Actual and Artificial is what the Strategy Buddha calls AI^2. It enhances our humanity and makes us more human.

You are equipped with the tools to create and reach your compelling future.

Strategy Buddha wishes you well and looks forward to guiding you on your journey.

Meet the Strategy Buddha

You will be guided on your path to enlightenment by the Strategy Buddha who understands the nature of the StratNav within you and will ensure you make the most of it. Strategy Buddha is a strategic pragmatist who will enable you to experience life differently. The life of Strategy Buddha has included senior roles in global companies, tech start ups, consulting in a global firm, military reservist, Diplomat, mentor, coach and has been on a journey to over 77 countries. The Strategy Buddha brings a balance of logical and spiritual thinking and will guide you. If you enjoy this book you are invited to connect with Strategy Buddha for further guidance on how to deploy the insight and be part of the community.

Strategy Buddha is your partner and your guide on the journey. It will enable you to define the destination, map out the route, develop the skills you need to arrive safely and the equipment you need to take. You will travel light, you will travel as a team and you will reach the place you foresaw in your vision.

Compass Mentis

If 'Compos Mentis' means 'having control of one's mind,' then *StratNav* is 'Compass Mentis' having control of the process to program it with intelligence and spirituality, and how to use it to get to your compelling future.

It's more of a guidance system than a compass and it requires you to take ownership. Strategy Buddha can explain the tools and techniques, but you will be required to add the missing ingredient that makes it unique to you. This is how you will give the StratNav a 'human nature.' We all have our own needs, desires, emotions and energy. Strategy Buddha will guide you, but ultimately it is you that must decide which journey and which path you must take. In the world of the StratNav it can best be described as 'Feel the Future.' An emotional attachment to a greater future that you engage with actively today.

Each of us will have to take ownership, create the vision, be prepared to learn. Ultimately, it's the actions you take that will determine the results. Strategy Buddha will be there for you as your guide. You will reach the summit and you will BEcome the person you decided you need to be.

In a world of challenges and opportunities we need a new guide to thinking strategically. In the world of logic, *StratNav* may appear to be just a concept or a framework— it's not. It's much more; it's mindset, and a higher level of intelligence to help you make full use of your brain. Your logical brain will find comfort in models and checklists. It is this thinking that has led to 90% of companies failing to achieve all their strategic objectives.

It's what people have thought 'being strategic' is all about. That's partly due to the fact that business education still teaches the classic models, and for many business schools it's a core part of the curriculum. The more enlightened schools and the true innovators will be reinventing the way we learn how to think about business. The classic models need to be applied better and re-evolve to take account that human beings are emotional, and rational expectations are not always the norm. Rational expec- tation is an enshrined assumption in most economic theories. In the world of leadership, we have the famous 'Situational Leadership' model from Hershey & Blanchard. Perhaps it's time for a model of 'Situational Strategic-ness.' *StratNav* will not bombard you with all the strategic tools. Rather it will help you learn how to think, use your brain to focus, analyse a situation, identify the future, select the right tool and move towards the goal.

ANOTHER WAY
OF THINKING

Coaching is Buddhism

In the world of the Strategy Buddha there are 8 steps to Nirvana.

I'm going to demystify the world of strategic thinking. It's only dull when you make it dull. You are right to think that it requires logic, checklists and project plans with detailed metrics and design, but you will also be aware that pilots experience a real joy when they fly above the clouds. You are the pilot of your vehicle of choice and you are going to need every insight you can find. You'll also need a flight plan and safety checks, fuel, crew, food... you get my drift.

Let me explain why I talk about emotions. You may wish to understand their origins, their meaning and how to understand them. I believe that transformation is akin to Buddhism. Let's take a look at the core elements of Buddhism so that you can see the relevance to reinventing or creating your business.

Core elements of Buddhism and how that helps us in business

If you struggle with this 'touchy feely stuff,' then now is the time to dive in. Strategy Buddha outlines the core principles of Buddhism and relates them to business.

Coaching and Buddhism are essentially the same thing.

The 4 Noble Truths

After enlightenment Buddha stated these 4 noble truths.

They are about changing your perception. Your ability to see things as they really are, not your opinion which may have been programmed into you when you were young. To become a Strategy Buddha you will need intellect, patience and be willing to embrace your true self. Once you've done that then you will be allowed into the 'store room' to select your equipment for the journey.

1. Life is about suffering and a general feeling of dissatisfaction.

2. Suffering comes from desire. The desire to meet expectations.

3. If we remove our desire, we will remove suffering.

4. The 8-fold path. This is the route to reduce suffering.

Buddha says that to be enlightened you need to understand two things:

1. the 4 Noble Truths

2. dependent origination.

Everything is a result of something that happened before.

What is 'Dependent Origination'?

In other words, nothing appears spontaneously as it comes from an earlier situation. A loaf of fresh bread is the result of flour, yeast, water and other ingredients to produce a tasty experience. This principle applies to everything... even you. You exist because your parents created you. Most of us, therefore, began as a thought before we actually existed.

The same principle will apply to your business. The quality of the original thoughts will determine the end results. You can link this to chaos theory which talks about the butterfly flapping its wings in London and creating a storm in China. Why not turn this principle to your advantage in the same way you can use the placebo effect to your advantage when it comes to engaging with your brain?

The key message is that if you can follow the 8-fold path to enlightenment then you will remove suffering and attachment. In this case it's an attachment to an old way of thinking that has not been serving you well. It's also attachment to a job or a business in which you have given yourself a job.

When you realise that everything is linked to everything else you start to notice the 'big picture' and the quantum or micro level.

Strategy Buddha will talk of the 'Golden Thread.' It's why Buddhism is a way of life rather than a religion. The thread is the core element that links your daily habits with your long-term vision.

The 8-fold path to Nirvana

As with any good business model (no disrespect to Buddha) it's not about the individual parts but the way they interact and combine to produce more than the sum of the parts. In reality it's not a path but a collection of elements that act as a set of fundamentals that are a set of guidelines. The word 'right' is used to mean a balanced view. It's the feeling you get when you say, "I don't know why, but things just felt right."

Using these fundamentals plus best practice in business will get you to your compelling future more rapidly.

1.   Right Understanding

This is about seeing things as they really are and not as we'd like them to be. It assumes a level of acceptance, awareness and pragmatism and these three things will help you with strategic thinking. If you learn this element well you will hold the key to experience reality. If we get this right, we avoid ignorance. Strategy Buddha believes that risk is the absence of knowledge. It's only risky if we don't understand it. Therefore, to master the StratNav you must learn. The master knows he is always the student.

2.   Right Intent

This is about commitment. Its aim is to help you decide and choose what you really want. It's heartfelt and you 'feel it in your heart and soul.' To be committed means that you not only know your 'WHY,' but you have passion for it and you have true grit or persistence.

If you are going to climb Mount Everest, you start at basecamp. You still need the will to do it, the map, a route, the kit and a Sherpa. *StratNav* is your strategic guide and pragmatist that will tell you the truths you need to hear.

> Note: Mastering these first two elements will help you lessen desire as you are merely getting on with your mission in life. There's no desire, just action.

3.   Right Speech

The words we use and the way we communicate them are important. This relates to the words we tell ourselves with 'self-talk' and the way we talk to others. It can relate to the way we communicate our strategic vision, objectives and goals to our team so that they have something to engage with.

4.   Right Action

The world needs us to protect it. It's time we did the 'right thing.' That may be subjective but *StratNav* works best when you have an ethical approach. This means honesty, no killing, stealing, sexual misconduct, drugs or alcohol that might impair your ability to achieve results that benefit the world. *StratNav* requires you to state your values and live your life using them.

5.   Right Livelihood

Put simply, try not to own a drug den, an underground off-license or a brothel. Avoid the slave and drug trade and do something good for your community. Establish good habits and rituals in your day that signify you are on a journey. Strategy Buddha knows that life can be tough and does not seek to judge, but he wants you to commit to a compelling future.

6.   Right Effort

Again, put simply this means have a positive attitude, have good intentions, control extremes of emotion (control your chimp) and be focused. How many books are sold to help people with this and nothing is implemented? Simple not easy.

Strategy Buddha knows that hierarchy is not the answer as these things are about human behaviour.

7.   Right Mindfulness

Mindfulness is one of the most powerful skills you can learn and develop. There is no past, there is no future. There is only the present. When combined with the other elements it makes sense to really focus on what you are doing. Even better when what you are doing is the right thing to get you to your Nirvana.

Strategy Buddha wants all *StratNav* users to be experts in Mindfulness. He has seen the benefits for himself and it can be transformational. It's a key part in implementing strategic changes in a business. Strategy Buddha gives you 24/7 mindfulness.

It's not about isolating yourself. It's about engagement with team, customers, suppliers and partners. With awareness you are able to change things; it is therefore essential to embrace change management—it's not 'woo-woo for the tree huggers,' it's how your human physical brain works and is the efficient use of the StratNav. You will learn to embrace change so that you are powered change.

8.   Right Concentration

With a clear strategic vision, a well written plan and a clear path to implementation, the right people, tools and processes, we move beyond agile. Imagine that you work efficiently on the right things with absolute clarity and focus. This is flow.

If you also look after your mental and physical health you will be invincible. You will then be ready to graduate to the 'sweet shop' full of all the strategic business tools available. You will come to them with a deeper level of understanding.

"Attitude not Altitude," as Strategy Buddha would say.

Wow... what a journey.

If this is all too much for you then that's OK. It's a journey and you now have a guide.

You can achieve an exponential growth if you know how to:

– select the right things to work on.

– Work on them in the best way.

I think we might assume that Peter Drucker was in fact an 'accidental Buddhist' when he talked about, "Management is doing things right, leadership is doing the right thing."

StratNav enables you to do both simultaneously. You don't need to choose.

Note: When you have mastered your mind and your body using the 8-fold path you will be ready to use the StratNav. Notice we have not yet talked about the 'four-box matrix' of the four-letter behavioural profile. All these things have a time and a place. Show patience. You don't need to be defined by them. In fact, it's the opposite. You have more control than you think when defining and moving towards a compelling future. You may want to explore issues more deeply. In which case Strategy Buddha encourages you to complete that work.

If you can focus on the right things in the present you will not be weighed down by the past nor fearful of the future. Why would you when you are working on the very things that will take you from pain and towards pleasure?

That is how you are released from the cycle of suffering and attachment. When you stop living in the past or the future you are no longer defined by time. This also allows your true spirit to come to the fore. It was already there, you just didn't notice. You have started the process of creating your very own time machine.

Your Strategy Buddha will enable you to take ownership of your future, teach you how to integrate the eight elements into building a business that you are not attached to.

The Strategy Buddha adopts the '8-fold path to Nirvana' (yep... the band stole the name). If you don't take the time to understand the role that your mind is playing in your lack of success, then don't dismiss the tools out there that you might think are 'woo-woo' or wacky. Take it from neuroscientists and successful people from some of the best academic institutions in the world. This stuff works if you learn, embrace and apply it.

There are many great tools in the strategic analysis and planning world so *StratNav* will enable you to select the right one at the right time. This is critical as too many people rush to deploy a tool that is not right for the job. You may find a tool that works, or you may need to create your own.

Strategy Buddha: "It's the soft stuff that's the hardest."

StratNav is 'tool agnostic'

You don't need to shave your head and live in the temple to be a Strategy Buddha so let's focus on the practical aspects of *StratNav*.

Creating a Compelling Future (RAS)

"Don't even think about it," said the Strategy Buddha when he met the Managing Director. The company had been in business for seven years and was about to bring in the 'Consultant' who they thought was about to show them the way to the future.

Strategy Buddha knew that the MD and the Consultant were already programmed to follow a path that was the wrong one for the company. In fact, the reason they had lost their way is that they didn't have a guide and were applying outdated thinking to the formation of strategy. They were about to repeat the mistakes of millions of companies.

Strategy Buddha knew the true meaning of the phrase 'put your mind to it.' What does that actually mean? Which 'mind' will you actually use?

We know from research by the Brightline Initiative in partnership with the Economist Intelligence Unit that 90% of companies fail to implement all their strategic objectives. Yes, 90%. That means you have a one in ten chance of achieving all your objectives using the 'tried and tested' tools. The reality is, they are 'tried and tested'... to not work.

This is why Strategy Buddha is on a mission to transform the consulting industry. It's why major consulting companies are moving toward the planning and execution stages and creating strategic ideas that are more likely to get implemented. This does not mean they are playing it safe. It means they are learning how to plan and implement great ideas. As Henry Mintzberg once said: "Strategic Planning is an oxymoron." It's clear that we know the results even before we've started as companies are following the well-trodden path to failure. Is this why the failure rate of business is so high?

It's time for a new approach to change. One where you accept that change is perpetual. It requires better strategic thinking skills and more engagement so that destinations are reached more often and more effectively.

When you 'think' you are doing 'the right thing' it's hard to step back and think about how you are thinking. In fact, some of you are getting agitated right now because you want to 'get on with it.' Is that you?

There is a scientific basis for this concept in the incredible work of the Flow Genome Project which tells us that the state of flow involves the brain doing less, not more. It switches off the usual functions that might slow you down and your brain literally gets on with things without friction.

As the Chinese
say… "slow down
to go faster."

WELCOME TO THE LAW OF PROPULSION

'Perpetual Coherence'

Brain scientists talk about 'Coherence.' The world's best at applying this science in a practical way is John Assaraf. It's a wonderful place to be because as John Assaraf says in his book *Innercise*, coherence is when:

> "your brain works like an orchestra. One that plays well enough together so that when you follow habits and think and act in alignment with your belief patterns and emotions, you can play some decent music. We call this coherence. For the brain,

coherence represents the ideal state of safety and efficiency. When your brain is in coherence, it thinks all is well, there's music and the gorilla is happy." (John Assaraf, *Innercise*, 2018)

If you try and change the script that is driving your behaviour you are creating a state of dissonance. As John Assaraf says, the brain detects that you are trying to change, it acts to 'protect' and it acts to save energy. After all, there is a switching cost in terms of energy and your brain is there to keep you safe and save energy.

Coherence is also a term used in cardiology. Dr. Alan Watkins in his book *Coherence* defines it as "a healthy amount of stable, predictable variability." He talks about a pattern of "energetic variability to deliver optimal performance." He goes on to say that, "physiological coherence is facilitated by cardiac coherence, therefore makes psychological coherence possible." In essence the many organs of the body synchronise with the heart as the lead organ.

Strategy Buddha would call this body and mind in perfect harmony. Imagine that you achieve coherence in both the mind and the body, then combine the two to create a state of coherence squared.

Strategy Buddha is on a quest to bring your mind to a place of 'perpetual coherence.' Imagine a place where there is no dissonance, no resistance. You are able to move rapidly to a new destination. There would be no fear, no doubt, no need for motivation, no need for willpower and the end of the imposter syndrome. Is it possible to have the duality of coherence of the mind and coherence of the body? If these two systems are then synchronised does that provide the ultra-high-performance state?

It sounds extreme but in reality, once you know how things work then you can train them so that it appears as if things happen seamlessly. Strategy Buddha suggests you explore the field of neuroplasticity as this is a key part of the Law of Propulsion; the ability to achieve goals rapidly.

You will embark on a journey of physical and mental fitness where the two work together to create exceptional levels of performance. Perpetual Coherence is probably what the actor Bradley Cooper experienced in the movie *Limitless.*

"The act of defining
your potential
creates a limit."
Strategy Buddha

If you are aligned with your true identity, then you have already defined who you are, and you move directly to that being. Once you have learnt how the StratNav works you can then can act with intention. For this to happen your Reticular Activating System (RAS) needs to ensure alignment between your conscious and subconscious; in this situation there is also no need for the 'imposter syndrome,' it's the intelligent use of emotion as opposed to emotional intelligence. You are in control, you have the destination and you have the guidance system. It's a mix of logic and spirituality and it makes you feel more human. To explore this field in greater depth Strategy Buddha recommends you read the work of Steven Kotler and Jamie Wheal from the *Flow Genome Project; The Art of Impossible* which is a blueprint for flow.

The latest research in brain science looks at how emotions are made. Dr. Lisa Feldman Barrett explains how emotions are built. In her research she does not refer to emotions being the result of a trigger. She describes it as prediction, that happens so rapidly, it appears as if it's triggered. Imagine, instead of a trigger response, you determined the nature of that built response.

If you think being an 'agile' thinker is cool, you are going to love *StratNav*. For *StratNav* takes you beyond merely being agile. *StratNav* will take you beyond the reactive and somewhat passive nature of the term agility and the concept of attraction, implied in the name. That somehow things will magically manifest themselves just by thinking about them. I mentioned the founder of Neurogym, John Assaraf, earlier as he will say that you must always "take action." In fact, the last six letters of the word say it all: attrACTION.

We start to explore the Quantum Mind. If a quantum computer can crack an encryption code instantly then a Quantum Mind can create the right thinking and get things right. What if we are able to create the 'Quantum Mind'? No more 'fail-fast' as we constantly hear from the online gurus. In a future of rapid, accelerating and perpetual change we must 'learn-fast.' Before we delve deeper into the Quantum Company in another book, we will take the time in this book to explain the role of the StratNav, how it works and how you can make best use of it.

A re-evolution is what it truly means to be strategic; for too long it has been seen as the Holy Grail of business, with vast sums of money paid to external forces to bring in quick fixes and instant answers. The reality being: massively complicated change programs that are great on process and weak on content and meaning or purpose. They have the impression of progress and certainty whereas the reality is, they are myths, delusions and rabbit holes. This is why 90% of companies fail to achieve all their strategic objectives. There's no point in being a 'black belt' if you are working on the wrong thing.

You are the 'missing ingredient'

What they lack is the human element. The 'missing ingredient' that only you can bring. It is unique to you and the situation you find yourself in. As the Strategy Buddha will prove, it's all about discovery and enlightenment. There is no instant answer, just a journey that starts with the right questions. In order to find that missing ingredient we need to 're-evolve.' That's a revolution that retains what works and brings some new thinking and insight to an existing tool. *StratNav* can only take you so far on the journey it helps you create, you will need to retain a growth mindset, be curious and keep asking the right questions.

Strategic Alchemy of Feminine Energy
– The basis of creation

When we focus on the utility of things we are looking at life as an economist. In life we require a combination of masculine and feminine energy. This is not a simple male/female thing. They are not in conflict and there is no need for dominance. If we look at everything from the perspective of economics, then it means the focus is on survival, when we should be even more creative and strategic. As an economist you will focus on the marginal utility of each additional input into the process. What if we can break free from the Law of Diminishing Returns and create perpetual value? For me, being strategic is about creativity and energy. It requires balance.

In the natural world we see this balance as the basis for life. It's only in the mind that we create this false distinction. This in some way explains the failure of strategic change. We are relying too much on logic, masculine energy and survival. It lacks the collaborative element of competition. It ties in with the concepts of scarcity vs. abundance or fixed mindset vs. growth mindset. Strategy Buddha calls for a rebalancing.

With feminine energy we talk about all embracing not all conquering.

Strategy Buddha
is a disciple of
the great Indian
mystic, Sadhguru.
You are advised
to seek him out.

Indian Alchemy is about making an element into something finer. It's about turning a stone into the divine. It's not the traditional western view of transforming things into gold. It is a consecration to turn ordinary things into fine things. How cool is that? It's about exuding a more subtle form of energy. Consecration is turning powerful energy into a more subtle form. It's transformation, as opposed to transaction. Where there is a transaction, then it's a zero-sum game or just a simple exchange. One person's gain is at the expense of another. This creates friction. Let's adopt the mindset of Abundance.

We need more co-operation, integration and 'one-ness.' When we combine, then we are recognising the very nature of existence and creativity. Some of you will view this through a religious lens whilst others will use a spiritual or energy-based lens. This may be too deep for some, but this is a key part of the StratNav and the Law of Propulsion. It's all about using energy and action to create a compelling future by taking action. This balance creates more energy and creativity which leads to the formation of objectives and aims that are aligned with the dynamics of an industry and a market. In some cases, it will lead to a disruption in the existing rules of a market or industry.

The source of energy is the 'Temple.' The Temple is a body and not a place of worship. We come to the Temple to be energised. Once you have 'been to the Temple,' you can transfer that energy into the StratNav to power the propulsion. Karma literally translates as 'action' or 'doing.' When people talk about Karma as, 'getting back what you put out there,' they are right.

Karma is a Kosmic Boomerang!

We see this in strategic change. It's time to embrace the spiritual and the emotional within existing strategic tools.

Agile

Agile thinking suggests you are reacting to things—when we react we have lost ownership and control. In fact, when we react there is no guarantee that we are not simply being triggered into a default response that has a high failure rate. Our brains think they are being triggered as it all happens so fast. The latest brain science is telling us that we are not triggered. It turns out that our emotions and how we feel about a situation are built. They are built in the moment and it happens so rapidly we believe it's triggered. Our brain only experiences something in as much as it's experienced it before. It looks for the information that is closest to something you already know then it builds an emotion for you. It's guessing. It means we can get things wrong, we can think we know what is going on and it all seems familiar. It also teaches us that sometimes we see something, and we don't know what it is. Welcome to the idea of 'Experiential Blindness.' If you wish to explore this area you should read the work of Dr. Lisa Feldman Barrett.

If your mind is guessing based on what it already knows, why not clean out that reference point and change the building blocks of your emotions? This will lead to better predictions by the brain as you have trained and conditioned it for your advantage.

It's when you look at something and you dismiss it as a wild dream or something unobtainable. In many cases you are just not able to envision any sort of future. Even worse, you just don't know how to create a vision of the future. You literally stare into space and you can't envisage a compelling future; you have no idea what it is; you have no experience of it. This is why you'll sometimes say to yourself, "I'll never get that," "I'll never be able to do that," or, "I don't know what to do," or, "I can't ever see that happening." This is when most people give up. The sheer scale of the gap between 'there and now' is too much and the brain defaults to its sole purpose. It is here to help you survive and ensure your body does not waste energy.

What if you can ensure your brain is working to your advantage, after all, it's inside your skull so it only knows what you tell it? Why not make it easier for your brain to build the right emotion and ensure you take the right action to get you there quicker?

What you need is a 'golden thread' that will connect you to the future. In reality this will be a system of habits and activity that, over time, will get you to the goal. So, 'experiential blindness.' It's only when you are given a little more information that your brain has something to compare it to; you then store that information in your brain ready for future use.

So why not give yourself a chance and start programming that reference place in your head with something so it appears more tangible and attainable? Because your brain is not able to distinguish between reality and a story of the future, you need to give it something to latch onto. This is the purpose of tools such as vision boards and affirmations. You need a device to help you filter things and decide what to 'pay attention to.' It's the reason you tend to have the same reaction to things and behave in the same way—it's what you might call 'familiarity.'

You can go one step further to propel your mind into the future by creating a dynamic film of your future with music, affirmations and images. You can also create a vision board based on the personality traits you wish to develop. This all leads to an explosive cocktail to propel you like a missile to the destination.

With *StratNav* you are creating 'future familiarity' and helping your brain choose what it pays attention to. However, when you know how to change the programming of the 'device,' you will be in control of one of the most powerful forces in the world. Under the Law of Propulsion, you are creating a 'hot spot,' which is your future; you then lock on like a heat-seeking missile and initiate launch.

We are human beings not human doings.

It's time to redress the balance. It's not the 'Law of Attraction' it's the 'Law of Propulsion' whereby you combine the physical, psychological, emotional and spiritual. Add to that the importance of a balance in masculine and feminine energy and you have the basis for a new way of thinking... literally.

With the Law of Propulsion, you choose the place you want to be; you determine what that looks like and you focus on that with all your heart, soul and intellect. Once you 'lock-on' to that future, set a course and lift-off, then *StratNav* will propel there. Think of *StratNav* as a catalyst, a tracking device, guidance system and mentor. As you guide it will also speak candidly and tell you the truth that it will also take focus and hard work. You will develop resilience, you may make mistakes, but you will learn to re-focus and restart the StratNav. Strategy Buddha will be your guide, your coach and your mentor.

The Law of Propulsion (LoP)

The Law of Propulsion combines the world of strategic thinking, positive psychology, mindset, mindfulness, health, transformation, strategic change and implementation. Strategy Buddha believes that the concept of 'attraction' is static and leads people to expect that things will 'come to them.' He wants you to flip this and use the principles of therapy and psychology to enhance and turbocharge the journey to your compelling future.

Why wait?

The field of Time Line Therapy typically:

> provides one of the most powerful processes and techniques for personal change and growth by facilitating the elimination of the painful emotions attached to memories or events in the past. TLT also focuses on what we can learn from those events and use what we learn as a resource for the future. Time Line Therapy techniques and practical processes produce long-lasting transformation much quicker.

> TLT is invaluable in enabling individuals to resolve negative emotional issues from the past and clear limiting beliefs and decisions that may have prevented them from moving forward as well as achieving their goals for the future.

Strategy Buddha has taken the principles of TLT so that the process now adds to the transformation journey and speeds it up. LoP enables you to attach pleasurable emotions to future visions. It's using TLT to accelerate into the future rather than only removing things in the past. The reality is that you may need to move backwards on your 'timeline' first to remove any weights or hindrances before heading into the future.

Sling Shot to the Future

Place yourself in a comfortable capsule, sit tight, strap in, and imagine you are now sitting in a 'sling shot' device. You will be pulled backwards initially, and this is to clean up any limiting beliefs. For some, this will require deep reflection. For others it will require therapy. The process makes you lighter, more focused and ready for the journey. It's an essential step and it's a chance to lighten the load by 'dumping the baggage.'

You now focus on where you DO want to go, what you DO want to do, and you achieve wisdom that will inform the journey. Imagine feeling calm, strong, focused and a sense of living your purpose. It's time to be fired up and channel that energy.

A firework is full of promise as it's launched—rising into the night sky and releasing its load of complex powders. Sadly, as beautiful as the explosion is, it is only a single event. It then burns out and the pieces fall to Earth. It remains a mere memory.

StratNav gives you a launch pad, a flight path, a guidance system, propulsion, in-flight refuelling and a navigation tool using telemetry to reach the target in the most efficient way.

I return you to the principle of AI^2. All this technology is great as it accelerates the process and the results. This is fine if the thing it is accelerating is robust and heading in the right direction. Before adding Artificial Intelligence, you must first use Actual Intelligence. Call this common sense, critical thinking, or the human spirit. Whatever it is, take the time to open your mind, scan the environment, discover new insights and learn new things. Create a set of parameters that act as your filter and a set of rules to help you change your trajectory. This means you are the 'missing ingredient', and you have to design your compelling future and prepare for travel. Once you do this you can use the technology and the tool. *StratNav* requires more humanity not less. It is a powerful tool and needs to be handled properly. *StratNav* is a 'special force' which requires training, learning, practice and patience. We all have the 'core technology' within us already and it has created the life you have today.

In the past many people and companies have been misguided. The irony of the word will not be lost on the disciples of the Strategy Buddha. People have failed to take the time to analyse, be creative and listen to their intuition about the future of their industry or life. In many ways people rush off in the wrong direction, with the wrong tools and vehicle and are not always aware they are even doing it. The feeling of movement becomes confused with direction and purpose.

It's akin to setting off on your round the world trip in the wooden go kart you built from old bits of wood and pram wheels when what you needed was the latest Toyota Landcruiser or Land Rover. Perhaps you require the Typhoon fighter jet or the latest spacecraft from Elon Musk or Richard Branson.

You miss a step in the process in your rush to get your hands on the 'shiny new object' and the strategic tool you think will give you the answer. It only encourages you to conform to traditional thinking which is proven not to work. You bring your existing experience, mindset and knowledge and assume that the future is merely an extrapolation of the past. You will end up repeating the same thing and falling into the trap of expecting a different result.

Strategic Pragmatist

I'm going to teach you to be what I call a 'Strategic Pragmatist.' It's about being creative and then applying it. That's innovation. You may not get it right first time but in the future with the Quantum StratNav you will. In a world where 90% of businesses fail to implement all their strategic objectives I'm going to ensure you are in the top 10%. In fact, I'm going to do more than that.

The ultimate aim of this book is to equip you with the mindset that will enable you to operate the tools to ensure you build a business that works without you. We will transform your 'busyness' into a business. One that works for you, has value as an asset and provides the life you really want. *StratNav* forms the basis for a new business model beyond agile. It is the route to the Quantum Company.

We begin with 'Feel the Future' and creating the 'golden thread' that links today with that vision of your ideal business. It's time to get comfortable with the uncomfortable as you work on your mindset and your business.

Being strategic is inherently a creative, intuitive and emotional process so try not to stifle it with too much logic at first. After all, you are designing the future so you're going to have to be ready to flex. I'm going to teach you 'how to sail' but I can't predict the weather with a 100% accuracy. Whilst I can help you define the destination and map out a route, ultimately you are the captain of your ship and you will have to navigate the realities of the high seas when the time comes.

Strategic thinking is about shaping the future of your business. It's about you as a leader and it's about the team. Strategy is about winning. This means it's creative, pragmatic, intellectual and challenging. It's about grit and determination to execute but also having the wisdom to alter course in the face of reality.

It's that fusion of creativity, insight, expertise, innovation and execution that positions you better than anyone else in your marketplace. You are playing to win. First you must choose the game.

We begin with questions. As the great Allan Pease might say: "Questions are the Answer."

How good do you really want to be and what does life and business look like when you get there?

Before we fire up the StratNav you are going to have to review your mindset, your thinking, your beliefs, your values and your skills. For these are the things that determine your behaviour, your actions and ultimately your results.

THE PROBLEMS
WITH BUSINESSES

UK Companies: Why
do so many fail?

McKinsey & Company talked about the 'Profit Curve.'
This shows a distribution curve of economic profit
across sectors where only 8% make the transition from
the mid-section to the super-profit section. The point of
strategic analysis to find hard-to-back-out-of choices about
how and where you will win. Planning is about how you
will make them happen and it outlines your strategy. But
in strategic discussions, we often miss out the thinking
and go straight to execution. We call it strategic but it's
really just taking action—it's a common error.

It might explain that, of the 6m companies registered in the UK, only 8000 employ more than 250 people. That suggests companies are not scaling up and are short lived. 80% fail within 5 years and this number has been steady for decades. In fact, if your company survives into a tenth year, it will be part of an exclusive club—'The 4 Percenters,' that is, only 4% of companies survive that long.

StratNav will ensure you learn from the past in the same way computers evolve using machine learning. The world of learning and development in the corporate world is ever changing and that pace of change has accelerated in 2020. Instead you need a StratNav to guide you. As previously discussed, *StratNav* is a set of principles that will not only help you define the future but provide a tool to navigate in an adaptive way; some of you may call that 'agility.' I believe there is a world beyond agility that is not reactive. It's not based on 'search,' but 'discovery.'

Search is limited by your own intelligence and beliefs. Discovery is able to explore and exploit information and help to define the right questions and the patterns that we can use to guide ourselves into the future.

Why 90% of companies fail to implement <u>all</u> their strategic objectives

This figure comes from the Brightline Initiative. The research was undertaken by the Economist Intelligence Unit and The Project Management Institute. Here are some other shocking statistics which the Strategy Buddha sees as evidence for a new way of doing things.

–   60% of firms struggle to bridge the gap between strategy development and its practical implementation.

–   The average company fails to hit 1 in 5 of its

strategic objectives.

- 90% of companies fail to achieve all of their strategic objectives.

- 53% say this execution weakness puts them at a competitive disadvantage.

Strategy Buddha sees part of the solution is the blending of consulting and coaching skills.

After all they are two of the six key leadership skills and leadership is a key part of being a strategist. Let's take a look at the six core leadership skills based on the work of Goleman, Boyatziz and McKee.

Strategic Thinking and Strategy Creation require Leadership

The Six Emotional Leadership Styles

Daniel Goleman, Richard Boyatzis, and Annie McKee described six distinct emotional leadership styles in their 2002 book, *Primal Leadership*. Each of these styles has a different effect on people's emotions, and each has strengths and weaknesses in different situations. Four of these styles: Authoritative, Coaching, Affiliative, and Democratic, promote harmony and positive outcomes, while two styles: Coercive and Pacesetting, can create tension, and should only be used in specific situations. Goleman and his co-authors say that no one style should be used all of the time. Instead, the six styles should be used interchangeably, depending on the specific needs of the situation and the people that you're dealing with.

> Note: You'll be able to choose the best style to use if you know how to 'read' others and the situation you are in. This is where it's useful to improve your listening skills, learn how to understand body language, and improve your emotional intelligence. Strategy Buddha will make use of behavioural profiles such as DISC and Wealth Dynamics to help you understand yourself and others so that you can engage in more productive conversations.

Let's briefly examine each style.

1. The Authoritative (Visionary) Leader

People using the Authoritative leadership style are inspiring, and they move people toward a common goal. Authoritative leaders tell their teams where they're all going, but not how they're going to get there—they leave it up to team members to find their way to the common goal. Empathy is the most important aspect of Authoritative leadership.

2. The Coaching Leader

The Coaching leadership style connects people's personal goals with the organisation's goals. A leader using this style is empathic and encouraging and focuses on developing others for future success. This style centres on having in-depth conversations with employees that may have little to do with current work, instead focusing on long-term life goals and how these connect with the organisation's mission. This style has a positive impact on your people, because it's motivating, and it establishes rapport and trust.

The work of Michael Bungay Stanier is essential reading for anyone serious about developing this skill.

3. The Affiliative Leader

The Affiliative leadership style promotes harmony within the team. This style connects people together, encouraging inclusion and resolving conflict. To use this style, you must value the emotions of others, and put a high value on their emotional needs.

4. The Democratic Leader

The Democratic leadership style focuses on collaboration. Leaders using this leadership style actively seek input from their teams, and they rely more on listening than directing.

5. The Pacesetting Leader

The Pacesetting leadership style focuses on performance and meeting goals. Leaders using this leadership style expect excellence from their teams, and often the leader will jump in himself/herself to make sure that goals are met. The Pacesetting style doesn't coddle poor performers, everyone is held to a high standard. While this can be a successful style, it can have a negative effect on the team, leading to burnout, exhaustion and high staff turnover.

6. The Coercive (Commanding) Leader

Coercive leaders use an autocratic approach to leadership. This style often depends on orders, the (often unspoken) threat of punishment, and tight control. People in modern, democratic countries are used to having a level of control over their lives and their work, and this approach deprives them of this. What's more, because this leadership style is so often misused, it can have a profoundly negative effect on a team.

Why Strategic Initiatives Fail

Before we unleash your inner-propulsion unit, Strategy Buddha will look at why strategic change has failed in the workplace. The research is overwhelming and there are lessons to be learned.

Here are the core reasons why 90% of companies fail to implement all their strategic initiatives. Reading the list of barriers to successful implementation and what can be improved tells the Strategy Buddha that people fundamentally do not understand the real nature of strategic thinking, planning and execution. If strategic skills and engagement levels were improved, we would not have such a failure rate of companies.

1.   65% of companies said that strategy falls short because of a failure to understand the company, its market environment and its ability to execute. This is the most shocking finding as that is what being strategic should be about; as in marketing, the ability of a company to define its position in a future environment is essential to being strategic. As Charles Darwin teaches us, it is the most adaptable that will thrive. Read the reason again. It says that executives don't fully understand their own company. This is further backed up by research published in the Sloan/ MIT Review that shows 51% of the executives in 4000 companies were not clear of the 'top 3' strategic objectives. How can you expect to guide the company, track progress and encourage engagement in that situation?

2.   The single most stated improvement was coordinating those that design the strategy and those that deliver it. Can you remember working at a company where the 'strategy' was just

presented to you and you were invited to attend a senior management presentation to announce a new initiative with a cool code name? It also occurs when companies bring in the 'strategy consultants' to create the plan. It looks rigorous and based on reality, but rarely is it something that can be implemented easily. Part of the solution is to create insight and change teams that are also tasked with implementation so there is more incentive to think about how it will work in practice.

3.   The CEO is actively involved. It's not just a project they sponsor. The iconic lone figure of the leader giving his blessing for a 'strategic review' that will report back in 6 months for his sign off is a thing of the past. What if CEO meant Chief Engagement Officer, Chief Empathy Officer or even Chief Execution Officer? Strategy Buddha directs you to the OKR practitioner's school. The Objectives Key Results model is based on systems thinking created by Intel and was then developed by John Doerr. He was the first investor in Google and the mentor to the founders. In his classic book, *Measure What Matters*, John outlines a new approach to performance management, goal tracking and engagement.

4.   People in the organisation must also contribute to the evolution as well as the implementation of strategic goals. Levels of employee engagement are estimated at 14% by a Deloitte/Gallup report. The earlier you can involve employees in the strategic thinking process the more robust will be the outcomes. This is because the diversity of mindset, experience and perspective create a series of options grounded in the real world. As

these options are screened and then translated into plans by the same people the probability of success in execution increases.

5.   It's not top-down or bottom-up. It's more meet in the middle, and it's dynamic. This is a core element of the OKR framework adopted by progressive companies and is the secret to a learn fast culture. It's the actual process of corporate telemetry which enables the people to change trajectory or stay on course as quickly as possible.

6.   Not tracking the reality and dynamics of the marketplace. Failure to track the changes in customer needs and changes in behaviour. This ensures that a flexible rhythm of meetings with hierarchy will allow resources to be reallocated to where the return on investment is highest. This will also apply to people and requires a new approach to performance management.

7.   Getting distracted by short-term metrics and goals. Known as short-termism, it prevents companies from taking steps that create a sustainable business that generates recurring revenue but has a high asset value with an above average valuation multiple.

8.   The implementation is not bold enough, it's too complicated and not focused enough. A strategic transformation involves exploring the scale, scope and significance of the organisation. Avoid incremental thinking or simple extrapolation of the past trends. Seek audacious goals that induce excitement and some trepidation.

9.   Team engagement is low and there is not enough cross-functional cooperation. Forward

looking companies are adopting the principles of OKR. The 'Objectives Key Results' mindset and toolkit enables companies to increase levels of engagement, ensure strategic objectives are the basis of everyone's decision making and activity.

10. Companies try to do too much at once which means that some initiatives are not completed before new ones are started. It is better to have fewer goals that everyone can align to and understand.

11. The culture does not always allow for mistakes or setbacks. It's neither culture of fail-fast nor learn-fast. There needs to be a culture of safety. In his book *The Culture Code*, Daniel Coyle cites this as one of the most important requirements. Safety enables people to raise questions, suggest ideas and be honest with each other without fear.

12. Failure to split apart the current activities of the business and treating the new initiatives in the same way as a mature business. In order to transition to the future, you need to nurture projects and assess them with a different set of metrics.

13. Success and wins are not always celebrated, and this is key to signalling that things matter, new behaviours get rewarded instead of ridiculed. Major transitions are comprised of numerous small wins so make sure you celebrate and reinforce them all.

A NEW KIND OF BUSINESS

Quantum Company

What is the world of the 'Quantum Company'? Think about it. If a quantum computer can decode an encryption in a flash, then what if you could apply that principle to a business? This will be a subject of another book by the author and will explore the concept of 'Quantum' in marketing, strategic thinking, teams, finance and operations.

If you can master the thinking required to focus and take the right action then you may be able to create teams faster, create instant customers, predict financial success or failure and even create instant strategy. 'Fail-fast' would become a thing of the past and the strategic thinking would be perpetual. Perpetual motion will power the culture and the engagement of the team and ensure everyone is aligned. The future is about 'learn-fast' and build as you go.

Strategy Buddha is a disciple of Jonathan MacDonald, the man behind *Powered by Change*.

You will know the StratNav is fired up and working when it has locked on to a compelling future. *StratNav* is no mere compass that tells you which direction is which. It's an integrated guidance system that uses universal and actual intelligence to define the destination, create a route, design the vehicle and then get you there in the most efficient way. The Strategy Buddha will not only enable you to find that compelling future, he will require you to be open minded, creative and vulnerable. The StratNav will ensure you pick the right path, take the right tools with you and make sure you track things as you go. You will not have all the answers at first, but you will have all the questions. You will learn to handle uncertainty, ambiguity and doubt before eventually finding a powerful level of confidence and certainty. You will feel it when *StratNav* is working.

Not only will you have a set of significant personal and business objectives, but you will have all the other elements that we typically associate with this: a plan, a vision board, a learning list, a peer group, atomic habits, a guide and a set of affirmations. Those typical things you may have been exposed to.

StratNav will
ensure that you
Feel the Future.

Feel the Future – The Golden Thread

StratNav nirvana is when you 'Feel the Future.' It's a powerful force in the present that links you to that compelling future. What links the present with the future is the Golden Thread. I call it the 'Golden Thread' because it's that core idea, that essence of a campaign or a design that defines it. It runs through the veins and it's a core element to keep you on track. It links everything you do today with the medium and long term so you stay on track. Its corollary is when you think back to an incredible experience in your past and it makes you feel good. Those 'chemical memories' are reignited and you feel great.

Imagine a rug maker who has a vision of the Persian rug. As he sits in front of his frame he adds one thread at a time. Each one alone seems insignificant but as time passes the pattern in his mind emerges and becomes reality. The 'Golden Thread' is the theme or the defining pattern; it's the DNA that builds the framework and the system you require to reach your end point. In business it's the way in which your daily activity across the term is aligned to the future. For the master artisan he knows what the end result will look like and he knows what each stage looks like. It's a journey made up of many small steps.

You will be familiar with the concept in habit No.2 of Stephen Covey's book, *The Seven Habits of Highly Effective People*. The idea of 'start with the end in mind,' has new meaning when you think about it in the context of the StratNav. Perhaps the new mantra is, 'end up with what you have in mind.'

It's how you ensure your 'Atomic Habits' and schedule used on a daily basis are linked to the weekly, monthly, quarterly and annual activities. Strategy Buddha suggests you become a student of the work of James Clear, the author of *Atomic Habits*.

As you will see, *StratNav* is an all-encompassing paradigm that pulls together traditional and contemporary strategic and tactical elements in the world of the Strategic Pragmatist.

To accelerate your learning and implementation of the concepts of *StratNav* you are directed to one of the most advanced, comprehensive and powerful business growth platforms. It is the basis for implementing many of the principles of *StratNav* and will give the tools you need to implement this new approach into your business. You can access it at: www.poweredbychange.com

Strategic Telemetry vs. Compass

It's telemetry, such as when you move forward, you are aware of where you are in relation to the destination and whether you need to take corrective action.

For many people and companies, they may be weaving a rug, but they have no clear picture of the end result and the final pattern is a mess. In some cases, they are using the wrong materials, have no process and are not building a business model or framework. They don't even have much training and were not mentored by a master. **StratNav will not only help you in your approach to thinking strategically, it will be your guidance system, dashboard and route map.** A compass won't be enough. You need a means to get to your destination by the most effective route possible. Imagine knowing that everything you are doing now will bring you a step closer to your compelling future. *StratNav*, once the emotional fuel tanks are full, then switches to a more technical and logical approach.

This is essential for the execution phase of the strategic change. In too many cases objectives are set, plans made, and implementation plans kicked off. The results are poor according to the Brightline Initiative which shows 90% of companies fail to implement all their strategic objectives.

Like any great guidance system, it will have a great dashboard that the owner can check in real time to make sure things are good. *StratNav* has the power to alter course so you do not drift for too long. It will use constant feedback and Actual Intelligence. In practice that means:

–   clear vision, mission and values

–   defined objectives

–   robust strategy

–   list of tactics.

To ensure all this works it requires a dashboard and a rhythm of meetings with key people.

You don't want to be a maverick with your future and you don't want to make it up as you go, so *StratNav* will empower you to move forward with confidence. **It combines intuition and logical thinking to create real strategic insight.**

If you are to climb a tall building, wouldn't you like to make sure your grappling hook is locked in, well positioned and able to take the strain? When it does, you simply reel yourself in without distraction. Those of you with fertile minds will be taking this analogy to the extreme so make sure it serves a purpose and is working for you.

StratNav brings intuition, intelligent emotions and represents a balance of feminine and masculine energy. *StratNav* brings the word love into the mix too. Perhaps in the future in a world of Quantum Computing and AI hyper algorithms we might see a machine capable of strategic thinking, but for now *StratNav* represents the power of the human being. It will engage with technology where it supports discovery and learning.

AI²

StratNav is the antithesis of these AI based machines that have 'superintelligence' and teach themselves without human input. *StratNav* is an 'AI based technology' by which I mean it's based on Actual Intelligence using the technology of the human brain and mind. *StratNav*'s future will evolve using AI². That is, we start with Actual Intelligence of people and then we turbo charge it with Artificial Intelligence. (AI².) For now, *StratNav* will enable you to tap into your natural intelligence and intuition. It will give you an energy, a clarity and focus like no other device.

A Journey of Discovery

Let me be clear. StratNav is here to help you be more human not less. It is this omission that is the root cause of 90% of failure in implementing strategic goals. By placing too much emphasis on logic and models, it **results in poor engagement, lack of flexibility and failure.** It's time to reclaim the human spirit. *StratNav* has learned from the concepts of AI and machine learning without complicating it and will provide you with your own form of 'deep learning' and will use a human approach to 'reinforcement learning.' This is defined as the balance between exploration (of uncharted territory) and exploitation (of current knowledge). *StratNav* calls that... discovery.

StratNav celebrates the human spirit and is about discovery not search. We search for something when it's missing. With discovery we merely see what was already there, but we were not open to its existence. With discovery we adopt a growth mindset and do not limit our beliefs or suffer from confirmation or any sort of bias. We discover we can initiate a process of creation. The creation and attainment of your compelling future.

Next Practice vs. Best Practice

To borrow a phrase of one of my all-time favourite strategy gurus, Prof C K Prahalad it's about 'Next Practice' not 'Best Practice.' I heard him speak at an event at the London Business School. It was the start of a brief relationship prior to his death but it left a major impact on my thinking. If you want to learn about the latest proven approach to creating the future, you can do no better than read the work of the incredible Jonathan MacDonald in his book *Powered by Change*. It's based on his intellect and his work with companies such as Apple, Ikea, Google and many more.

He gives you a toolkit for a visionary.

You are going to need to step into your courage zone as that is where the growth comes from. The StratNav will be your guide but it will also be a candid friend that tells you the truth. You need to hear the truth so that you have awareness, are open to learning and are not tied up in ego and desire. This is where the 'Strategy Buddha' will help you with his StratNav or internal guide.

Whatever you tell me about the current state of your business, *StratNav* will always look for evidence of the results before you move ahead or change direction. In the

Courage Zone, *StratNav* speaks the language of the truth. It may use intuition, but that will be backed up with evidence and a 'learn-fast' mentality. It will allow you room for ambiguity and uncertainty but when required it will be candid; giving people the truth from a heartfelt place is where the growth comes from.

StratNav will not join you in a pity party. It ensures you define the end point then gets you there quicker. *StratNav* is a way of thinking to ensure you avoid the 90% failure rate of others. It is your guide and your mentor as well as your coach so that you define and realise the potential yourself.

Do you ever hear a voice asking: "is this as good as it gets? How great can it be? How good do you want to be?" Who do you need to BE to achieve your objectives and dreams?

Together we will bring the latest brain science, psychology, thinking on mindset and business acumen and tools. My fellow traveller, this is the genius of the StratNav. Not only does it allow us to revisit the past, it takes you into the future in a way that you can make sense of now. I call this experience 'Feel the Future' or 'Timeline Strategy' and I'll show you how you can experience that.

It will be like being sat in a sling shot that pulls you back briefly then… let's you go, getting propelled forwards. Latest brain science suggests that emotions are not triggered but that in fact we create them. This suggests we have more control than we think. Strategy Buddha directs you to the work of Dr. Lisa Feldman Barrett, *How Emotions are Made.*

Imagine what you could achieve if you weren't restricted by things such as 'limiting beliefs,' 'imposter syndrome,' and all those other terms we have been conditioned to look out for and realise. They say 'ignorance is bliss' but what if you were able to rapidly learn and implement so that you turned into a sort of 'time machine?' It would be as if Elon Musk was your therapist and you came to the conclusion that it is possible to move at very high speed in a dedicated tube without friction. This is the 'hyperloop of strategic thinking' that is possible.

When you are ready to graduate you will be introduced to how to use *StratNav* to create the Quantum Corporation. One where the terms 'Agile' and 'fail-fast' become obsolete. We leave the Law of Attraction and adopt the Law of Propulsion.

To Do vs. To Be

How you perceive, view and think about something determines how you feel and act. Is that true or do you agree that feelings come first?

Perhaps it more a case that what you have in your subconscious determines how you think about something and perceive it. You are in effect not watching, you are projecting what's inside. The emotions that we feel are actually created by us. Our brain is taking a guess at which emotion it will build in the moment. Because this happens so rapidly we think that we are being triggered or we are reacting. With a fully functioning StratNav you will go deeper and write new code that is the building block of the emotion.

It is said that, "seeing is believing," which suggests that external things impact on us and then we accept them and that until something is 'real,' we will not accept it. You have more control over things in life than you realise. No longer will you be a victim of your emotions or fate. Instead you will learn how to define your aims, direct your mind and control the energy, directing it where needed to get results. As you develop competence with the StratNav, your confidence will grow.

The Stoic, Marcus Aurelius once said:

> "The things you think about determine the quality of your mind. Your soul takes on the colour of your thoughts."

Strategy Buddha will teach you that 'believing is seeing.' You start internally with a vivid view of your compelling future, imprint that into the StratNav, and then it will manifest or materialise. The reality is, it requires learning, planning, action and hard work but at least you will know it is taking you to the right destination.

Not only is *StratNav* a guidance system, it also acts as a filter. With clear goals you have clarity. With clarity you know what to focus on. When you are met with the volume of 'noise' and information you will automatically tune in to what you need. You will be familiar with this concept in the field of bias. It's called unconscious bias because we have embedded it so deeply we are not aware of it. Once we have awareness we can move to a neutral state. From there the StratNav is gradually reprogrammed with intent. It's no longer an automatic bias, in the negative sense, it's now a highly tuned, intuitive and aware state.

For example: in business we often hear people say that the issue needs a 'helicopter view.' It implies that you need to step back, take yourself out of the situation or that other well-known phrase, 'can't see the wood for the trees.' In that case why not build a tree house and 'see the wood from the trees?'

Strategy Buddha wants you to literally come up with a **compelling future** that is 'out of this world.' In order to create that you need to view the situation from a long way off. A helicopter or even a satellite is what we call 'Geo stationary' as it maintains its position in the gravitational pull of the earth.

You need to get out of the gravitational pull of your current location and get to a place far enough away to change your thinking. Are you familiar with the reaction of astronauts when they see the Earth for the first time from space? For many, it's life-changing. For others it's a religious experience.

This is what Strategy Buddha has in mind for you.

The Overview Effect

According to Wikipedia it is defined as:

– a cognitive shift in awareness reported by some astronauts during spaceflight, often while viewing the Earth from outer space. The most highly trained people on the Earth experience it and the earlier explorers did not anticipate it.

– The effect was first explained and concept coined in 1987 by Frank White, who explored the theme in his book *The Overview Effect: Space Exploration and Human Evolution.*

This quote by an astronaut on Apollo 11 captures it nicely. The same mission that saw the first man on the moon.

"The thing that really surprised me was that it [Earth] projected an air of fragility. And why, I don't know. I don't know to this day. I had a feeling it's tiny, it's shiny, it's beautiful, it's home, and it's fragile."

Michael Collins, Apollo 11

In late 2019 it was reported that researchers at the University of Missouri aimed to reproduce the experience, with an isolation tank, half a tonne of Epsom salts, and a waterproof VR headset. These same floatation tanks are used by England rugby players to recover more quickly and by Navy Seals to help them learn languages more quickly. It's not woo-woo, it's brain science and related to the different types of brain waves. If you would like to learn more you should check out the work of the Flow Genome Project who are world leaders in this subject matter.

The Overview Effect in your business

What if Strategy Buddha could enable you to experience the equivalent of the Overview Effect with your business? By looking at something from far enough away you change your mindset. Or perhaps you simply reset your mind. How can you look far enough into the future of your industry and market to see the position of your future company?

Strategy Buddha uses a process of visioning the future that is both scary and exciting. Of course you can't do it with existing skills, knowledge and resources. If you could you would have done it by now... wouldn't you? That's just a task isn't it? Yeah right. We'll take a break and come back when you've had time to jot down your thoughts.

You'll be using a range of tools and I highlight one process called 'Elevation' which has been used by the guru Jonathan MacDonald. It's led to innovations and trans-formations that will have already impacted on your life. If you want to learn more then check out his work in *Powered by Change*.

> This is what strategic thinking is all about. It's a creative process which is also highly structured which means you don't need to be an eccentric or a creative type. Instead of relying purely on logic you will open your mind so that things unfold. It releases you from your attachment to the past and the present.
>
> Strategy Buddha at his best.

After that, you need to learn how to create a pathway to get there, program the StratNav to guide you and make sure you stay on target. I've simplified the process but with all the knowledge we have about business and mindset do you think we can create a new paradigm? Strategy Buddha does just this.

The Strategy Buddha is called into many soul-less companies that have lost their way. They exist but have lost focus, purpose, energy and dynamism. Something is not right. They have lost their spirit and their soul. They are also lacking a robust guidance, system, dashboard, strategic view and financial insight and control. They are effectively on life support and if one thing fails then it's likely to set off a chain reaction they are likely to die from. You will find that levels of engagement are low, and employees are not clear about purpose, plans or practicalities. Do you work in a company like that? Have you ended up creating a company like that and you'd like to do something about it?

Despite the fact that time does not exist they say things like:

- we are too busy

- we don't have time

- we just need more customers

- there's so much to do.

Such companies are full of 'human doings,' as opposed to 'human beings.' They have short term mindsets, thrive on 'To Do' lists, love long meetings, levels of engagement are low and even the leaders are not sure what the strategic objectives are. People are organised in groups, tightly controlled, performance and reward are not always aligned. The senior executives take a day out to agree values and then tell the staff what they are. They assume the future is an extrapolation of the present. This leads to boring forecasts based on extrapolation and a linear route to the future. In fact, they do not realise the difference between being strategic and having a strategy. *StratNav* will teach you 'backcasting,' not forecasting.

Why strategic thinking is not strategic

This misunderstanding of the words is one of the main reasons why 90% of companies fail to implement all their strategic objectives. Such companies believe that 'bringing in the consultants' will save them. Strategy Buddha has been a management consultant and he likes to think of it as bringing in a 'hit and run' driver to teach road safety. The driver gets a joy ride and gets back on the road but can leave a trail of destruction behind him.

It's like being taught to drive by someone who has covered up the windscreen and only allows you to use the rear-view mirror. You end up basing your strategic thinking on a small percentage of the view which is in fact, watching the past. You may think you know how to drive but as you accelerate off in one direction you soon find out how that particular 'strategy' ends up.

Make the MOST of your vision

This simple acronym will literally help you make the most of your business. Your Vision is an inspirational view of the future. It's how you see your business in the future and it's what you want it to be. It will involve intent and purpose.

M. O. S. T. – Mission Objective Strategy Tactics

Mission: tells you what you do at the core to achieve the vision.

Objectives: what is it you want to achieve? It's your goal

Strategy: It's quite operational and is merely the way you will approach the objectives.

Tactics: these are the actions you take.

Running a business using unclear objectives, poor tracking systems and 'To Do' lists will just wear you out. It's draining because you are just running around doing stuff that's not linked to anything. You are lacking purpose, meaning and focus. This is where you need the Golden Thread. Strategy Buddha calls that a 'busyness' and the person that started it is merely the owner of a job. They are not the owner of a business and are 'paid' accordingly.

StratNav will enable you to make the transition to a company, run by its 'To Be' list. It's based on that thing called Vision. That 'fluffy, woo-woo-thing' you dismissed because you had 'stuff to do.' I prefer to think of it using the words of Steven Kotler, in his book *The Art of The Impossible* who would call it 'Massively Transformative Purposes' or MTP. A company vision is the result of thinking, feeling and creating the future. You have to step out of the day-to-day business and take some time. The word vision asks you to define what you want to see in the future. Too many people rush to dive into actions and end up killing creativity and great ideas that might mean the difference between success and bankruptcy. A typical 90-day period in business is approximately 540 hours. Do you think it's worth spending 1% of your time working on designing the future and working your way to it? That means you spend just over half a day making sure you are on track every 90 days.

Prior to that you can engage in a process of 'Elevation.' An innovative process that will enable you to define your business in a way you never thought possible. Strategy Buddha directs you to the work of Jonathan MacDonald, *Powered by Change.*

You may also be familiar with the concept of flow. Clearly a state of flow has implications for the Time Lord. If you are able to experience time differently and achieve extraordinary levels of performance then you need to understand flow. Strategy Buddha guides you towards the work of Jamie Wheal and Steven Kotler and the Flow Genome Project. Their world-class research provides practical insights into how to achieve flow.

The initial insights came from the work of Maslow. Well known for his research and the term 'self actualisation' but his work was mostly about the concept of 'peak experiences.' At the time, much of the thinking in psychology was about 'extrinsic motivation' with the simple premise of need and reward, i.e. people will do one thing to get another.

It seemed that much of the thinking was about how to 'fix' things rather than explore possibilities. This led to Maslow's focus on 'intrinsic motivation'. Instead of mystical experiences he talked of peak experiences. In his own words:

> "the individual experiences and expansion of self, a sense of unity and meaningfulness in life. The experience lingers in one's consciousness and gives a sense of purpose, integration, self-determination and empathy."

The idea of intrinsic motivation says that the reward is the experience of the state of flow for its own sake.

Maslow's work was built upon by Mihaly Csikszentmihalyi who was interested in happiness. It was him that gave us the term 'flow'. What he discovered after extensive research was this. The people that are happiest are the ones who had the most meaning in their life and the most 'peak experiences'. This is something we instinctively know is true and this has led to a whole new body of work to explore the concept of flow.

Flow is an essential state for the Time Lord and turning yourself into a 'time machine'. This may sound strange but it isn't when you realise that neuroscientists can now scientifically prove concepts such as 'transient hypofrontality' and the basis of the feeling of 'oneness', using a SPECT scanner which detects things in the part of the brain known as your OAA or 'orientation association area'.

Required reading for any Time Lord is *The Rise of Superman* by Steven Kotler. The following list can be found in his book and is the ten key parts of the flow state as defined by Mihaly Csikszentmihalyi:

1.   clear goals:

2.   concentration

3.   loss of the feeling of self-consciousness

4.   distorted sense of time

5.   direct and immediate feedback

6.   balance between ability level and challenge

7.   control (personal)

8.   intrinsically rewarding

9.   lack of awareness (of bodily needs)

10. absorption.

One major realisation is that flow increases your creative decision making skills so you are more likely to be getting things right. This has implications for the concept of 'fail-fast'. Perhaps we should focus on 'learn fast'.

You should also note that further work has been done on the concept of group flow which has implications on how we operate as teams.

StratNav is not going to give you more work to do. It's going to give you less. You will be more productive and as the owner you will be building a system and team that create the business that works for you and enables you to live the life you really want. It's time to Make a Life and banish the phrase, Make a Living.

When you exist in a purposeful company with a clear vision, mission and values you will be ready to become a 'To Be' based company. A 'To Be' organisation perceives time differently. You will reach a point where everything you are doing is optimised. Think of it as Business Mindfulness. You are doing the right thing and you are doing things right. There is no attachment to the past or the future. Strategy Buddha blends management thinking with ancient philosophy. To him, coaching is Buddhism.

It focuses everything on doing those things which bring the company closer to the objectives. Yes, it will require hard work, good management and a tracking system that adapts. It will have dashboards, targets, projects, forecasts and cashflow statements. In fact, it will appear to have many of the things you expect to see in a business.

A closer look will reveal it is fuelled by energy, creativity, insight and intellect.

A 'To be' based company knows that perception is the ability to see things as they really are, not an opinion based on little analysis.

What is different is the energy. The way people communicate, share information, make decisions, the rhythm of meetings, the level of engagement and the results will be driven by fundamentals of the Strategy Buddha. The culture is not just a list of traits to aspire to. It must be embodied by everyone so that it becomes the new norm. The other differences include the pace it operates at, how it learns, its view of mistakes and its ability to handle uncertainty. Yes, it might be more agile than the average company, but it is not reacting as the word 'agile' suggests. Instead it is in control as it is building the future.

You are starting to build the 'Quantum Company.'

> A Strategy Buddha is an 'Architect of the Future and not a defender of the decline.' It is on a journey to a place 'beyond Agile' which is not reactive. Ultimately it flows effortlessly and rapidly.

StratNav will enable you to turn your thoughts into results. "Oh yeah?" I hear you say. "Who is this 'Strategy Ninja?' Buddha, actually, to tell me about emotions and all that fluffy stuff." It's a natural response to something when you live in a world of unconscious incompetence. That's not me being rude, merely a term psychologists use.

STRATNAV

Where would you really like to go ?

StratNav contains the RAS

The Reticular Activation System is a part of your brain. You already own a StratNav. You just haven't been paying attention to it. Now that's interesting because the job of the RAS is to tell you 'what to pay attention to.' It's all about clarity and focus.

It has been proven to play a vital role with breathing, sleep patterns, heart beat, sexual arousal, waste removal, appetite and interestingly for Strategy Buddha, it brings things to your attention.

The very fact that you are reading a book about your RAS means you have started the process.

Can you imagine life without it? Do you think it might be worth learning more about it, how it works and how to deploy it to help you achieve your goals?

RAS/StratNav is a portal and it determines what your conscious brain focuses on from all the information in your subconscious. It's estimated that the subconscious can handle 400 million bits of information whereas the conscious mind can handle 2000. The StratNav is a selective filter and the good news is... you can program it.

Your job is to decide what the parameters are for your filter.

It's like having a GPS and search engine in your head.

It works in two ways. You can set the main goal and then allow the RAS to start work so that you start noticing the things you need. Or it will act like a heat seeking-missile to help you use your clarity to get there faster. It's not magic. You still have to write a plan, have a schedule, develop habits, learn fast, seek support and take action. As Jonathan MacDonald says in his book, *Powered by Change*, "you start to learn fast and not fail fast."

When you combine creativity, emotion, clarity, learning, focus and a strong belief system you have the most powerful tool in the world with *StratNav*. It's not in your hands, it's literally in your head.

You may have heard of confirmation bias and placebo effects. You are about to use these to your advantage and tell yourself what you want.

84

Who are you?

Like an iceberg, people will only see a fraction of you, and they will only see your behaviours. The actions you take, and the behaviours people see, are based on deeper, more fundamental factors such as values, beliefs, skills and identity.

Your belief system is vital as you will be filtering the world for evidence that what you believe is true. You may even dismiss signals (facts and evidence) to the contrary even though they might save you time, money, energy or heartache.

If you want to create fertile soil for your new affirmations, you need to go deep and start working on your self-image and what you believe about yourself. If you try to plant new vibrant seeds into concrete, they will not take hold and grow.

This is why many people who make affirmations or read that book about 'wishful thinking' then complain that nothing happened. Well, let me be candid. Nothing happened because you told your brain things that were not accepted, you didn't persevere, learn anything, or take any action. Before we plant the seed of a vision or an affirmation we have to look at our self-image and self-worth. The reader may want to explore the field of 'personal construct theory' to further understand the importance of the story we create about our identity.

The purpose of the StratNav is to tell your brain what you want. It's like putting the postcode into your car satnav. You'll get there quicker.

Chaos Theory talks about how the slightest change in the starting conditions of 'the system' lead to a dramatic impact on how that evolves. Because the StratNav is a catalyst it will get you there faster. This means you must spend time on preparation and choosing the right trajectory. This is vital to the Law of Propulsion because you do not want to end up in the wrong place more quickly. Chaos Theory is not as chaotic as the name suggests and the implications for business are as follows.

If you make a small change it can lead to rapid and vast consequences. Some of you will be thinking that this means that things go wrong but it can equally suggest that things go right. You read the sentence and you chose to predict a positive or a negative story. That was based on what you had already stored in your brain. In effect you made an assumption or a prediction.

Changing your beliefs is not simple. It depends on what you read, who you hang out with, what you learn, etc. Take the time to look at your belief system as it will determine the results you get. Believing is seeing. You must choose the response the situations you face so that you retain ownership to your being.

If you create the right belief system then when you plant the seed of the affirmation and you plug that into the StratNav, you will be more focused and get there quicker.

How to use the StratNav: Instruction

You've been using it for years. You just didn't realise it. Now that you have awareness, you begin to take control. Unfortunately, like many people, you've been telling it to pay attention to the 'wrong stuff' and that is exactly the stuff that you have more of. It's obvious. You told your brain what to focus on, and guess what? It did. So, when I asked you the question at the start of the book: 'Have you ever wondered why things never really turned out the way you thought in business or life?'

The answer is that things did turn out the way you thought. You were just thinking the wrong thoughts and were not aware of them.

Are you ready to learn how to take charge of your thoughts, to determine which emotions you feel and to take the actions that will get you to where you want to be?

StratNav is your new best friend so take good care of it.

Preparation for using the StratNav

Step 1 – ALIGNMENT - Decide on your destination.

At this stage you must only work on the end point, the goal, the aim, the mission. It's tempting to want to rush in and start taking action. You may hear this referred to as the 'WHY.' However, having an ethical and meaningful 'why' is not enough to sustain you when change is required. As Jonathan MacDonald says in his book *Powered by Change*, just being "clear about your 'why' does not automatically guarantee continued success in a perpetually changing world". We will talk later about the 'what.'

It's the reason for a vision and a mission statement.

> Vision tells you what you want to BE.
>
> Mission tells you what you will DO to get what you want.

It's also worth noting that sometimes you find it hard to think about the future as your search is limited by your current mindset. It likes the so called 'comfort zone' which is not actually that comfortable.

You need a way to enter the courage zone and you will not do it alone nor without learning. You need a way to think about thinking about the future. You then need a way to get there and the tools and data to tell you about your constant journey. An infinite journey.

This is where you will need learn about 'discovery.' It's about exploration. Darwin didn't just come up with his theory of evolution. He spent years in the field collecting data and looking at reality. It wasn't until he served his apprenticeship did he master his art. What you are doing to achieve mastery?

Discovery is creative, it's emotional, it adopts a growth mindset, looks for infinite goals and purpose. It's all about exploration. This is where you go wrong as your fixed mindset tells you that you don't need to learn and you don't need to be creative. You just need to pull yourself together, do some work and stick with those tried and tested methods. At this point Strategy Buddha is thinking, 'what tried and tested' methods?

It tells you that you have enough information already and so your existing RAS just goes off and looks for evidence to confirm this. You remain uncomfortable in the comfort zone. It should really be called the Familiarity Zone and what you are familiar with has not worked well.

This ends up as a downward negative spiral of fear, anxiety, denial and poor decision making. They say that stress makes you stupid. In fact, it just stops you from learning.

The Strategy Buddha will provide you with tools to help you explore the things you are proud of, create a bucket list and help you to discover goals of significance. If you are heading towards a compelling future.

Alignment Process

This is a key step in ensuring you choose the appropriate destination. This is the time to get curious about everything. The next few pages give you a taste of a few initial practices you can undertake.

Let's begin with PURPOSE. As they say, success doesn't happen by accident. You have to do it on purpose. Strategy Buddha has a simple exercise to help you define your purpose.

Take your time and let things unfold. Listen to your inner voice and your higher self.

Creating Purpose

1. Think of an occasion where you have felt at your best, where you were in flow, and that gave you a sense of deep fulfilment.

2. Describe the situation in as much detail as you can.

3. Describe the experience.

4. Describe what you were doing.

5. Describe how this is meaningful for you.

6. Repeat steps 1–5 two or three times for different occasions.

7. Once you have all the answers, take time to reflect and then complete this statement.
My purpose is…

Take time to feel comfortable with your answer. Once you are, then you are ready to move to the next step. If you are not ready then the Strategy Buddha recommends you engage with Myles Downey, one of the world's greatest thinkers and practitioners. His book, *Enabling Genius,* will be a part of your discovery process.

A: Personal Goal-Setting Exercise.

Ideally, take some time in a new environment to undertake this work. Remember that we are starting the process of creating your compelling future, initiating a shift in your trajectory. This is your opportunity to change the way you have thought, behaved and set a vision and goals.

This is a simple yet effective way to design the perfect life for you. Most people go through life without having clear goals and 'drift' from one week to the next. Invest some time to think about what you really want and then write it down. Follow this exercise from start to finish without skipping any of the steps.

Step 1

List five things that you have accomplished that you are proud of. Take note of the situation, how you felt and explore that for a few minutes. There will be some form of physical, emotional and spiritual memory. Aim to feel those sensations again. We will need them later

Step 2

Make a list of 50 most important things you want to achieve and accomplish in the next 10 years. The list should include things you would like to acquire, experiences you would like to have, places you would like to visit and so on. Be creative, imagine that you have all the time and money in the world to live your perfect life. This is a list of what you want, NOT what you think you can achieve.

Step 3

Against each of the 50 items indicate whether it is approximately a 1, 3, 5, or 10-year goal.

Step 4

From the items that are marked as one year select the top four. The four that are most important to you.

Step 5

For each of the four items write a brief paragraph as to WHY this goal is important to you.

Step 6

Describe the person you need to become in order to achieve all of the 50 goals. You may need to acquire more knowledge in a particular field, you may need to become more disciplined perhaps or more caring or even more open minded. Be honest with yourself...

Step 6.1

Look at your list every day and as you start to achieve your goals strike them off the list and add another one to take its place.

Some very important notes...

1. The reason WHY we want to achieve or accomplish something is more powerful than achieving the goal. Step 5 is a critical part of this process. This is the start of building an

emotional attachment to your compelling future.

2. Becoming the person you need to become to achieve the goal is more valuable than achieving the goal itself e.g., set yourself a goal to become a millionaire, NOT because of what a million pounds can buy you, but because of what sort of person you will need to become in order to achieve it.

3. Be careful of the person you become in order to achieve your goals.

B: Business Goal-
Setting Exercise

The main purpose of this first Planning session is to help you get clarity on what type of business you want to build, have a clear One-Page Strategy supported by a strong short-term plan of ACTION.

I hope you found the Personal Goal setting exercise useful as we want to make sure we build a business that will enable you to live the life you want to live. We start with the personal goals and then turn our attention to building a business that will enable it.

In order that we can get the best use of the time together, please give some thought to the following questions ahead of the session. They are intended to help you get greater clarity on how you want to see your business in the future.

Please think about a point in time perhaps between 3 and 10 years from now.

- How big do you want your business to be?
  - Sales
  - profitability
  - people
  - locations
  - net worth.
- What would be your core markets?
  - Geography
  - sector
  - product / service (s) offered.

94

- Apart from money/financial considerations why else do you want to be in this business?

- What type of 'culture' do you want to have in the business and why?

- What do you see your role being in the future business?

    · How many days per week do you want to work?

    · What (if anything) would you specifically be responsible for?

- In an ideal world what would give you a 'competitive advantage that would be near on impossible for a competitor to replicate?

- Do you have a desired exit strategy and date in mind? If so when and how?

- How do you want your team to describe what it's like to work in your business?

- How do you want your clients to feel about doing business with your company?

Don't worry if at this stage you're not able to fully answer all the questions; it's just the start!

STEP 2 – Load up the StratNav

Once you've found your courage, thought creatively, and analysed the opportunities you will start listing core personal and business goals. We will cover the business analysis aspects later but for now we will focus on the StratNav itself. We are focussed on who you need to become.

Once you have gone back in time and prepared your subconscious mind then you can start to make use of affirmations, vision boards and other tools to reinforce where you want to go.

WARNING: The Stratnav is a time machine that gets you to the destination more quickly. If you have not defined the destination nor prepared for the journey then you will get nowhere fast.

When used to its full capacity it has the ability to take you to the compelling future, fast. If you program it with vague thoughts and lack clarity you will end up all over the place.

Practical note:

Building a 'time machine' requires patience, skill, intellect, energy and an open mind. Add to that list a set of 'blueprints,' the appropriate toolkit and the wisdom to deploy them in the right combination at the right time. To paraphrase the words of Peter Drucker, we provide ourselves with a core principle. Namely, we must do the right thing and we must do things right.

Strategy Buddha has been influenced by so many but when forced to state a few key tools the top three are as follows. The primary objective being to transform strategic thinking, communication, and execution through best practice in leadership and engagement.

1. Be 'Powered by Change'. Based on the real life work of Jonathan MacDonald with CEOs of many of the world's best companies. This framework epitomises 'AI Squared' and gives context for the StratNav to exist within.

2. *The Coaching Habit* is a best-selling book by Michael Bungay Stanier. Building a coaching culture into your business is essential because coaching is simply a skill of management and leadership.

3. OKRs: Objectives and Key Results are a powerful methodology that bring next practice to ensuring companies define their destination, track the journey and get there in the most efficient way.

There will be others, but these are three core tools in the armoury of the Time Lord.

Perhaps you feel that successful people are just more motivated, or they have some special skills. Perhaps they have more willpower. What if they had learnt to master their StratNav, learnt new skills, set the StratNav with the right postcode and were working to an efficient schedule en route to a compelling future?

Willpower is overrated. It has been shown to run out. Relying on willpower alone will not get you to the end.

Motivation too is overrated. Just ask Mel Robbins, author of, *The 5 Second Rule*.

James Clear in his ground-breaking book *Atomic Habits* says that the most important thing in achieving goals is creating a system of daily action to actually get results. Otherwise it's all wishful thinking.

Strategy Buddha's Advice: Stop, think, take time out and design a compelling future. Then tell your StratNav what to look out for, what it looks like and what it feels like. It wants to help you. Your brain is designed to help you survive and save energy. If that means making you think twice then you have to reassure it. Once you do this it will assume that what you are asking for is important and key to your survival.

If you get this right, then you will 'FEEL THE FUTURE.' This is the sign that your StratNav has accepted the destination. All you need to do is make sure you learn, do some work and have a plan and a schedule.

You might be reeling thinking about all that thinking, planning, scheduling. It's going to turn you into a robot or a machine. I don't have time for that... I'm too busy being busy. Instead, stop and think. You actually end up with a sense of freedom as you are not tied to a diary and a 'To Do' list. You are now en route to an exciting future. Your perception of time changes. You feel liberated from the clock as you know that you are doing the right things as well as doing things right.

This is your 'To Be' list and it will ensure you become the person you want and need to be. It will ensure you build the business that is an asset that pays you.

StratNav may be a physical part of your brain but it's fuelled by creativity, energy and visual elements. The emotions are created by your brain based on past experience, so you need to teach it some new ways. These then become the new reference point and go some way to removing the 'emotional blindness' we discovered from the work of Dr. Lisa Feldman Barrett.

Recent work by Dr. Lisa Feldman Barrett in her book *How Emotions are Made*, confirms the principle that we have much more choice than we realise. This means that if we can find the 'postcode' for our compelling future, teach our RAS what to look for, learn to slow down and be mindful, then focus our efforts we will end up doing the right thing and things right. It's a perfect combination.

Only then should you start to think about which 'Strategic Planning Tool' you need for analysis, planning and execution. Some of them will enable you to structure your thoughts and result in a plan that makes sense. One that is based on a vision of the future but maps out a clear pathway to the goal. When you have completed the exercise to design that compelling future we talked about you can take the next steps. This can involve:

–   vision board

–   affirmations

–   a dynamic movie

This is the core purpose of the StratNav. The wide strategic approach is the context into which the StratNav works.

This book has covered these core areas:

1.   the world has changed

2.   how traditional ways have failed

3.   introduced you to a new lexicon of strategic thinking and action

4.   how to use the StratNav

5.   a process to kick-start it.

This book's sole aim is to introduce you to a new lexicon, a new language, so that you can build your very own time machine. It is the start of a journey of discovery which requires you to be curious, learn, explore and experiment.

From now on
it's not 'seeing
is believing,' it's,
'believing is seeing.'

This is a book to introduce you to a new concept. If you embrace it, think about its message and start to test out some of the ideas you will notice the difference. In the spirit of evolution and learning the Strategy Buddha wants to hear your thoughts about the ideas and the impacts of applying them. Together we will take the lexicon and apply it in our daily life so that it becomes a new paradigm.

Strategy Buddha is exploring the world of the Quantum Company and you can be part of that tribe at www. stratnav.com.

Welcome to the world of the StratNav.

It's time the world adopted the Law of Propulsion.

It will change your experience of time and enhance you as a human being.

STRATNAV

A New Lexicon for Strategic Thinking

- Re-Evolution: a gradual transformation.

- Search vs. Discovery.

- Law of Propulsion: the new law for how proactive people get to their destination.

- Compelling future: a designed future you have an emotional attachment to.

- Strategy Buddha: your guide to using *StratNav* in your life.

- Quantum Mind: a mind that can make the right decision rapidly.

- Beyond Agile: the shift to a proactive strategic mindset.

- Be more human: ensure creativity and emotion are used in strategic thinking.

- Human Beings vs. Human Doings: a balance of emotion and logic.

- Golden Thread: the core theme that links the present with the future.

- Compass Mentis: directing the mind with intelligence and spirituality.

- Perpetual Coherence: a constant state of being in the mind-body connection.

- Hyperloop for Thinking: rapid movement to finding the right answer.

- AI^2 (Actual Intelligence + Artificial Intelligence): synergy in decision making.

- Feminine Energy.

- Strategic Alchemy: the ability to turn thought into wealth.

- Intelligent use of Emotion: learn to control your inner space and project.

- Feel the Future: the emotional link between the present and the future.

- The Missing Ingredient: only you can create the right solution for you.

- TO BE vs. TO DO.

- Believing is Seeing: you have more control than you think.

- Time Line Strategy: clean up your attachment to emotions about the past.

- Sling Shot: the process to propel into the right future at great speed.

- Unlimiting Beliefs: building affirmations and self-image to enable your strategy.

- Courage Zone: extend your comfort zone.

- Strategic Pragmatist: creative yet action oriented.

- Inner Game of Strategic Thinking.

- M.O.S.T: Mission Objective Strategy Tactics.

ABOUT THE AUTHOR

Richard Perry is a strategic advisor, mentor, author, NED and coach to business owners, MD's, entrepreneurs and CEO's driven by an unyielding dedication to ensuring they define and meet their potential. He is a Business Performance Coach that combines intellect, resilience, humour, creativity and humanity. An ideal guide in a time of uncertainty.

He is a High Performance Coach trained by the best and member of

- Powered By Change

- Flow Genome Project

- OKR Master Certification

He is a Strategic Pragmatist that combines being truly strategic and executing well defined plans that get results.

Richard has supported companies in over 50 markets worldwide, in the UK, Europe, Asia, Latin America and lived in Prague and Delhi. His methods and approach have helped clients expand into new markets, build high performance leadership teams, take advantage of profitable opportunities, improve productivity and increase revenue.

He was a Regional Director of AstraZeneca (Europe) and built the UK India Business Council in both countries. In addition he has spent time as an Army Reservist in 4 Para and held a Diplomatic passport.

Consultant at Bearing Point, where he successfully supported acquisitions and international expansion in emerging markets. He also provided strategic consultancy for Orkash Services India, assisting them in supporting governments, corporates and investors in critical projects overseas.

Richard holds a Masters in Economics and Management from the University of St. Andrews, and a Diploma in Business Administration and Management from Henley Management College. He is a certified business coach with Action Coach.

As well as completing the London Marathon in 2019 for Alzheimer's Research, he regularly completes charity Treks in London, Jurassic Coast and the Brecon Beacons over 26 miles.

If you want to know more, please contact me:

richardperry@stratnav.com

www.stratnav.com

Printed in Great Britain
by Amazon

67557779R00072

YOUR GUIDANCE SYSTEM TO A COMPELLING FUTURE

STRATNAV IS YOUR PERSONAL TIME MACHINE TO GET YOU WHERE YOU REALLY WANT TO GO FASTER THAN YOU EVER THOUGHT POSSIBLE.

IN STRATNAV YOU WILL DISCOVER YOUR INNER GENIUS GUIDED BY THE STRATEGY BUDDHA

"STRATNAV IS THE TYPE OF THINKING THAT CHANGES PARADIGMS. IT IS UNIQUE, ACCESSIBLE YET PROFOUND AND INSPIRES ME TO ACHIEVE MORE. STRATNAV IS THE TYPE OF THINKING THE WORLD NEEDS RIGHT NOW"

JONATHAN MACDONALD WINNER OF THE BUSINESS BOOK AWARD 2019 (EMBRACING CHANGE)

ISBN 979-8-59-260

WELCOME TO THE LAW OF PROPULSION....ENJOY THE RIDE

BEYOND

THE EYE

JEMA FOWLER